Made in the USA
Coppell, TX
20 July 2021

59245632R00063